Nutty Number Riddles

Natty Number Riddles

By Rose Wyler and Eva-Lee Baird

Illustrated by Whitney Darrow, Jr.

DOUBLEDAY & COMPANY, INC.,
GARDEN CITY, NEW YORK

Library of Congress Cataloging in Publication Data

Wyler, Rose.
  Nutty number riddles.

  SUMMARY: Mathematical riddles and puzzles to amuse and challenge young minds.
  1. Mathematical recreations—Juvenile literature. 2. Riddles—Juvenile literature. [1. Mathematical recreations. 2. Riddles] I. Baird, Eva-Lee, joint author. II. Darrow, Whitney, Jr., 1909–   III. Title.
QA95.W95   793.7′4
ISBN: 0-385-00602-0 Trade
      0-385-00685-3 Prebound
Library of Congress Catalog Card Number 74–33695

CONTENTS

6

COUNT UP
COUNT DOWN

But watch for twists and turns
in these nutty questions. They
sometimes lead to sensible answers.

Astronauts who travel in space
Come to an astonishing place
Where creatures tall and grand
Have twenty nails on each hand
Five and twenty on hands and feet—
And this is true without deceit!
                              Really?
Well, where do they land?

On Earth.
The creatures the spacemen meet are
you and me. Add a few commas to the
verse and the m[...] ach
of us has twent[...] and
five, and twent[...] et.

How can you tell the number of grooves
in a phonograph record without counting them?

How can you tell the number of records
in a cabinet without counting them?

A record has one groove and you don't
count up to one, do you?
A record made with separate grooves
could not be played continuously.

As to how many records are in the cabinet,
have someone else count them.

What is used in measuring that no one can
see or touch?

Numbers.

Think what happens when you measure ½ cup of milk. You put the milk in a cup with ½ marked on it. The half is a symbol that can be written ²⁄₄, ³⁄₆, .5, and so on. It is not the number itself.

Where is the number?

In the milk?

Fill the cup so that the milk comes up to the 1 mark. Does this mean you made the ½ disappear from the milk? Of course not.

The numbers you use in measuring do not exist by themselves. They are not real things. Like all other numbers they are ideas.

And no one can touch or see an idea.

How many feet are in an arm?

The answer is two if you use your own foot as a measure of your own arm.

The number of inches in a person's foot usually equals the number of inches in the forearm from wrist to elbow, and the forearm usually is the same length as the upper arm from elbow to shoulder.

Once upon a time there were two monsters.
One lived in a forest and it was little.
It was two times one-half its length.

The other monster lived at the edge
of the forest and it was big. It was
four times one-fourth its length. It was
much bigger than the little one.

How much bigger? Maybe you can tell.

The monsters had never met until one
day both of them decided to take a walk
in the forest. They first saw each other
when they were 300 feet apart. Each took
a deep breath and hissed. The big monster
gave a big hiss and the little monster a
little hiss. Then each moved exactly 150
feet. When they stopped, they were still
300 feet apart.

And do you know why?

Although the difference in their sizes was very great, you cannot tell how big the big one was. That's because everything that is long is four times one-fourth its length.

$$4\times\tfrac{1}{4}=1$$

Nor can you tell how small the little monster was because everything that is long is also two times one-half its length.

$$2\times\tfrac{1}{2}=1$$

These figures just say each monster was as long as it was long. Which it was, wasn't it?

Well, when the monsters met, the big one
moved forward 150 feet. The little one was very
frightened and it moved backward 150 feet.
Then the little monster turned and ran. It
ran and ran, going as far into the forest as any
creature could possibly go.

Now how far was that?

Halfway into the forest.
If a creature went farther than that, it would
start coming out on the other side.

1. How can you add five different numbers and get ten?
2. What number is neither odd nor even but written with one odd and one even?
3. What is the smallest number you count with—1, 2, 3, and so on—that can be written with two digits?

1. Here's one way:

   0+1+2+3+4=10

   Here's another way:

   ¼+½+1+1¼+7=10

2. A fraction written with one odd and one even digit, such as ½.

3. One.

   It can be written this way:

   1/1

   And this way:

What has eight legs and moves minus ten feet?

An octopus.

It's no trouble for an octopus to move minus ten feet, that is, −10 feet. Numbers with minus signs in front of them are negative numbers. They are sometimes used to measure depth, and so moving −10 feet just means going down ten feet below the surface.

There is a number—and it has a name—
That can be multiplied by any other
And still remain the same.
Divide this number any way you wish
And the number that you get
Will be the one you started with.

                  Which is . . .

Zero.

Remember, zero is a number. It is the one we use when there are no units to count.

Compare it with another number—for instance, six, which stands for a group of six units. Multiply six by two, and the result is the same as when we combine two groups of six units.

Divide six by two, and the result is the same as when we split the group into two equal parts and see how many units are in each part.

Now let's think of zero as a group of no units and see what happens when we multiply it by two and divide it by two. In both cases, the result is the same—zero.

How can you pick up a ton of coal by yourself?

Pick it up a pound at a time.

Who uses parts of dead people's bodies as measures?

You do.

You and the rest of the people living in the United
States use the English system of measurements, which
includes the inch, foot, and yard. These ancient
measures came into use over a thousand years ago.
The inch, it seems, was originally the distance
from the knuckle of a man's thumb to the tip; the
foot, the length of a man's foot; and the yard, the
distance from the tip of the nose to the tip of the
middle finger of an outstretched arm.

These measures varied from person to person, which
led to lots of cheating. Eventually one particular
person's measurements—those of King Edgar—became
the basis for the yard. The foot became ⅓ of a
yard and the inch, ¹⁄₁₂ of a foot.

The English system spread throughout the British Empire and at one time was in widespread use. But nowadays most countries of the world use the metric system of measurements.

In this system the standard unit is the meter, based on the length of a certain light wave. All small and large units are multiples of ten, and so 100 centimeters equal 1 meter and 1,000 meters equal 1 kilometer. Since the system is easier to use than the old English system, the United States probably will adopt it within the coming years.

MORTON, THE MORON

When people say he is a problem child, he smiles.
He thinks they mean he is good in arithmetic.

Morton is ambitious. He wants to get into high school.
That's why he carries a ladder around.
But why does Morton cut long pencils down to stubs?

He thinks he needs short pencils for short division.

One day his sister Cleo was helping Morton do his homework. He had to learn the number of days in each month.

"Thirty days have September, April, June, and November," she explained. "All the rest have thirty-one, except February. That usually has twenty-eight days but in Leap Year it has twenty-nine. Get it?"

"Yes," said Morton. "What do you think I am? A moron?"

"Well, tell me, how many months have twenty-eight days in them," said Cleo.

"They all do," said Morton.

When Cleo looked through Morton's school notebook, she came to a page of drawings, each with a number.

"What in the world are these?" asked Cleo.

"Answers to math problems that I made up," said Morton.

"These are answers? Where are the problems?" asked Cleo.

"On the next page," said Morton.

And there they were . . .

Morton's Math Problems

Did You Ever See . . .

1. . . . a decimal point?
2. . . . a division sign?
3. . . . a multiplication table?
4. . . . a boy measure two square feet?
5. . . . a teacher multiply?
6. . . . four take away three?

One day Morton started to cut up a dollar bill.

Cleo was very upset.

"You don't know what you're doing!" she cried.

"Of course I do," he said. "I'm dividing a dollar into four equal parts."

"Why, Morton? Why?"

"Four quarters make a dollar, don't they?" said
Morton. "And I need change."

Morton liked to use a ruler. One day he worked
for hours, trying to measure the letters on a page in
his arithmetic book.

"Are there thirty-six inches in a yard?" asked Morton.

"Yes," said Cleo.

"Then there's a letter that's always nine inches
long," said Morton.

"You moron," said Cleo. "A letter?"

"Yes," said Morton. "The letter Y. It's always a quarter of a yard."

Cleo was really worried when Morton started taking his ruler to bed.

"For heaven's sake," said Cleo. "Why the ruler?"

"Because I want to figure out something," said Morton. "I want to see if the foot on it is a right foot or a left foot."

"You moron," said Cleo.

But Morton continued taking the ruler to bed. He said he wanted to measure how long he slept.

Morton's next project was an invention. He worked
for days trying to saw an alarm clock bell in two.
He said he wanted to make a half alarm.

"What for?" asked Cleo.

"To wake up half of two people who sleep in the same room," said Morton. "Then one half can get up and one half can sleep."

"What if there's only one person in the room?" asked Cleo.

"The half alarm will wake up half of him," said Morton.

Cleo was about to ask which half. But she decided what was the use. Instead she said, "Morton, YOU MORON!"

RIDDLE TRICKS

Counters or props of some sort are needed for these tricks. Work them out first by yourself, then try them on your friends.

Sticks or toothpicks are the props that go
with this story:

Ho and Mo lived in cavemen days and used sticks for
numbers. One upright stick stood for one; two
sticks for two; and so on.

It seems Ho was not very good at stick arithmetic.
He had a lot of trouble learning to add and subtract.
While doing his cavework one day, he placed eleven
sticks this way:

$$|| - |||| = ||$$

"Something is wrong," Mo said. "The sticks read
two minus four equals two." Then he added, "But the
numbers will make sense if you move just one stick."

Do you see how the mistake can be corrected?

Arrange the sticks this way:

$$||=||||-||$$

Now they read:

$$2=4-2$$

Using toy figures or buttons for soldiers, can you
show how Sergeant Stiffstuff placed his twelve men in
six lines, each with three men in it?

Using toothpicks for boot polish, can you show how
Sergeant Stiffstuff divided a box of twelve closed bottles
equally among his men while leaving one bottle in
the box?

46

The sergeant lined up his twelve men this way:

Then he passed out eleven bottles of boot polish
to eleven men and gave the bottle left in the box,
along with the box, to the twelfth man.
Clever Sergeant Stiffstuff!

Do you ever play dominoes? Then you know the ends
are marked with numbers. A blank stands for zero
and each dot stands for one. In playing, the pieces
must be placed so that the number on one end matches
the number on the end it touches.

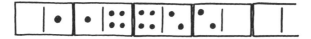

If you follow this rule, can you place the twenty-eight
pieces in a set of dominoes so they form a square?

Try this too. Placing the dominoes according to
the rule of the game, can you arrange the twenty-eight pieces
in a square with the same number of dots on each side?

(*Hint:* Each side will have forty-four dots.)

By the way, if you don't have dominoes, make a
set from cardboard and mark them this way:

Since there are twenty-eight pieces in a set, each side of
the square must have seven pieces.

It is easy enough to arrange the pieces end to
end with matching numbers if each side can have a
different number of dots.

It's much harder to make a square with the same
number of dots on each side. This can be done only
if the dots on the domino halves forming the four corners
add up to eight. Perhaps you can fill out the sides
of the square if you use a corner piece with four dots,
two pieces with two dots and one with no dots
(4+2+2+0=8).

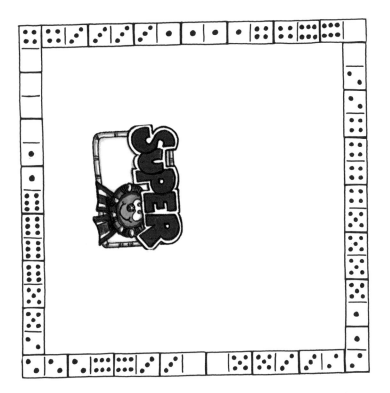

Here's one of the many ways to solve the problem.

Check the total number of dots on each side of the square and you will find it comes to forty-four.

Ready to put the dominoes away now?

Well, can you put all twenty-eight of them in two bags, each with more than fourteen dominoes in it?

Put all the dominoes in one bag and put that
bag in another bag.

Do you have a deck of playing cards? Then try this.
Can you pick out three cards and place them side by
side so they form a three-digit number that is divisible
by eleven?

The secret is to choose first and third card values that add up to the value of the middle card. For example, these three cards

form 385.
Divide 385 by 11
and you get 35.

Now for some number juggling. It's fun.
You will need nine slips of paper, numbered one
through nine.

See if you can juggle the numbers around so that
they form two straight lines, each with five numbers
that add up to the same sum.

Try this too. Can you divide the slips into three
groups, each of which adds up to the same sum?

54

When you juggled, did you get these results?

Here's an interesting way to play odds and evens.
Before you start say, "Let's do it this way. I'll
add my number of fingers to yours. If your number
is even, the total will be odd; if it is odd, the
total will be even."

Then both of you hold your hands behind you and
both show your chosen number of fingers at the
same time.

In order to win, how many fingers must you show?

Try another round and say, "Now it's your turn to
win. This time when I add my fingers to yours, if
you show an even number, the total will still be even.
If it's odd, it will still be odd."

And that's what happens because of the number
of fingers you show.

How many will that be?

On the first round show an odd number of fingers.
Odd plus even gives odd; odd plus odd gives even.

On the second round show an even number of fingers.
Or show a closed fist—in other words, zero fingers.

1. Draw a straight line on a piece of paper. Now can you arrange three pennies so that two heads show on one side of the line and two tails on the other side?

2. Lay down seven coins to form a cross like this:

When you count the coins, there are five in the long part and three in the arm. Can you move two coins and rearrange them so that both parts of the cross will have the same number in them?

3 How can you make a cross with just four coins?

1. Stand one penny on edge between the other two.
2. Take two coins from the bottom of the cross and put them on top of the coin in the center of the arm.

3. Hold the coins in your fist while you draw a cross. Then RUN!

WHAT GOOD IS A DEAD HORSE?

You probably have heard of the Noodleheads.
Nearly everyone has. But do you know the
story of the horses on Noodlehead Farm?

When Mr. and Mrs. Noodlehead were first married,
they had lots of different animals—pigs, chickens,
geese, cows, cats, and dogs. Yet Mrs. Noodlehead
was not satisfied.

"We have no riding horses," she said.

"I'll have to do something about that," Mr. Noodlehead
replied.

So he went to town one day, and when he came
back he said to his wife, "I have a surprise for you."

"What is it?" she asked.

"Look in the barn. There's a horse for every
day in the week."

"You mean you bought seven horses?" asked Mrs.
Noodlehead.

Then off she ran.

When she opened the barn, in front of her stood . . .

. . . only one horse.

Mrs. Noodlehead was very disappointed.

"Well," said Mr. Noodlehead, "you can ride him on Monday, Tuesday, Wednesday, Thursday, Friday, and Saturday."

"Oh dear," said Mrs. Noodlehead. "I wanted a horse to ride on Sunday, too."

In time there were more horses on the farm. The Noodleheads had three sons who took care of the horses and helped with the farm work. The family prospered.

Eventually Mr. and Mrs. Noodlehead decided they had had enough of farming. One day they told their sons they were retiring to travel and see the world.

"We are leaving everything to you," said Mr. Noodlehead. He explained that since the oldest had worked the longest, he was to have half of the animals and the land. The middle son was to have one fourth, and the youngest, one sixth.

Then off he went with Mrs. Noodlehead.

The brothers decided to divide the horses first. But how could they do this? There were eleven horses and three of them.

The brothers went to wise Farmer Brown, their neighbor, for help.

The oldest brother said, "How can we divide our eleven horses into one half, one fourth and one sixth?"

"Without cutting up a horse," said the middle brother.

"If we cut up a horse, we'll have a dead horse. And what good is a dead horse?" added the youngest.

"A dead horse can help solve your problem,"
said Farmer Brown. "I'll show you how. I just
happen to have a dead horse."

Farmer Brown brought the animal to Noodlehead
Farm and then divided the horses.

How did he do it? Well . . .

. . . he added his dead horse to the eleven, making twelve in all. Six—one half of the horses—went to the oldest brother. Three—one fourth of them—went to the middle brother; and two—one sixth of them—went to the youngest. One horse was left over. But that was the dead one which Farmer Brown took back.

The next problem was to divide the other animals. This was harder. There were thirty-seven chickens, twenty-three geese, five cows, one pig, one cat, and one dog.

The brothers went to Farmer Brown again. He told them to sell all the animals and bring him the money. The brothers thought this was a great idea.

They sold the animals for $2,300. Then they went back to Farmer Brown.

"Do you still have the dead horse?" asked the youngest brother. "If you do, we can add it to the money and divide it."

"No, no," said the middle brother. "That won't work."

"Help us, Farmer Brown," said the oldest brother.

Farmer Brown took a pencil and pad and
started to do some figuring. But when he tried to
divide the money into one half, one quarter and
one sixth, he ran into trouble.

"Look at these figures," said Farmer Brown.

$$\tfrac{1}{2} \text{ of } \$2,\!300 = \$1,\!150$$
$$\tfrac{1}{4} \text{ of } \$2,\!300 = \$\ \ 575$$
$$\tfrac{1}{6} \text{ of } \$2,\!300 = \$\ \ 383.33\tfrac{1}{3}$$

After looking at the figures, the oldest
Noodlehead said, "You are very wise, Farmer Brown."

"Indeed," said the middle Noodlehead.

"I guess you boys don't see what the problem is
now," said Farmer Brown.

"Is it that ⅓ of a cent?" asked the youngest.

"Not exactly," said Farmer Brown. "After each
of you gets your share, there will be almost $200
left over. And even if we divide that money
according to the will, there still will be some left over."

"Forget it," said the oldest Noodlehead.

"Dividing it up is too much work," said the middle
Noodlehead.

"Let's buy ice cream with the money," said the youngest, "and have a party."

Which they did.

And what a party it was!

After that the only thing left to divide was the land. But when each brother took his share, a narrow strip remained. It was half a mile long by three inches wide.

"Let me have it," said the youngest.

"What can you grow on a strip like that?" asked the oldest.

"Don't worry," said the youngest. "I'll grow— noodles!"

All kinds of problems come up in

SCREWBALL ARITHMETIC

For instance,
What Did They Say?
What did one ruler say to the other?
What did one decimal say to the other?
What did one calculator say to the other?
What did one angle say to the other?
What did one zero say to the other?
What did one arithmetic book say to the other?

Said the ruler, "It's tough when you can't make ends meet."
Said the decimal, "Did you get the point?"
Said the calculator, "People can count on us."
Said the angle, "We can be right but never wrong."
Said the zero, absolutely nothing.
Said the arithmetic book, "I've got problems.
How about you?"

A little wooden man stands on top of a cuckoo clock. Every time he hears the clock strike once and the bird call cuckoo, he jumps twice. The clock strikes the number of hours, every hour on the hour. When it is six, it strikes six times; at four, four times.

How many times does the man jump in 24 hours?

Since when can a wooden man hear?

Stations A and B are each at the end of a single-track railroad 120 miles long. At exactly the same instant, one train leaves A and one train leaves B. The engineer operating the train from A averages thirty miles an hour and the engineer on the train from B averages sixty miles an hour. Where will they meet?

In the hospital.

1. "He loves me. He loves me not," says the girl as she goes around a daisy, pulling off first one petal, then another.

   If the daisy has 63 petals and she pulls them all off, does he love her or does he not?
2. What should you add when you subtract?
3. If Farmer Jones sells 999 bushels of wheat at $7.77 a bushel, what will he get?

1. You can't tell.
2. A minus sign.
3. A Cadillac.

Can you figure out a problem using meters instead
of feet or yards? Well, try this one:

If you are blindfolded and move one meter to the
right and then move ⅔ of a meter to the left, then
go north for ¾ of a meter, where will you be?

In the dark.

What number is always in the middle of the telephone directory?
Where can you find seven digits that form sixteen?

One.
There are nine letters before and after o-n-e in
      THE TELEPHONE DIRECTORY
Count them!

On the telephone dial.
If you dial the seven digits in the number 749-8336,
you will dial the seven letters that spell
      SIXTEEN

Why are the numbers from one to twelve like good detectives?

Because they are always on the watch.

1. What is the lowest point a thermometer can reach?
2. How can you make a number smaller by adding to it?
3. When is a half not a half?

1. That depends on where it lands after you drop it.
2. Take a fraction such as ½ and add digits to the denominator. Say you add the digits 3, 4, 5. The fraction becomes $\frac{1}{2,345}$, which is over a thousand times smaller than ½, the number you started with.
3. When you take half of a quart of milk. You then have a whole pint.

   (Two pints=one quart)

What is it that a Frenchman will not touch with a
3.048 meter pole?

Whatever an American will not touch with a ten-foot pole.

In France people use meters instead of feet in measuring length, and in the metric system 3.048 meters equals ten feet.

Screwball Arithmetic is not new. Here are some old ones that were asked in your grandparents' and great grandparents' days.

1. What number can you give
   That never gets smaller
   As long as you live?
2. When can you be sure fourteen is the right answer?
3. A word I know, six letters it contains,
   Subtract just one and twelve remains.
   What is the word?
4. There sits two legs,
   Holding up one leg.
   Up jumps four legs
   And runs off with one leg.
   How many legs were there?

1. The answer to the first enigma
   Is the number of days since you were born,
   A number that can only get bigger.
2. When someone asks how do you pronounce
   F-O-U-R-T-E-E-N
3. You may think it's absurd,
   But "dozens" is the word.
   Take *s* away and there's a dozen
   Which equals twelve—
   Neither less nor more
   In any land, on any shore.

4. Two legs belong to a man
Who sits in a chair.
The leg he holds up is
A leg of lamb.
The four legs that jump up
Belong to a dog.
Now figure out how many legs that comes to.
Did you say seven? Wrong. The chair has
legs too, so the answer is eleven.

In Screwball Arithmetic problems are sometimes disguised. Here's a famous problem in addition in which each letter stands for a different digit:

Take the E, for example. Above or below the line it stands for the same digit, which is different from the digit N stands for. To solve the problem you must find the digits that stand for the different letters. When you do, you get a correct sum, which, in this case, is the amount of money wanted.

Start with S and M, and you see they add up to a two-digit
number. This cannot be more than nineteen. So M must stand
for one. Now the number added to one that gives a two-digit
sum is nine. (9+1=10) So S must stand for nine and
O for zero, giving:

```
    9 E N D
    1 O R E·
   ─────────
    1 O N E Y
```

From there on it is not hard to get the final result,
which is:

```
    9 5 6 7
    1 0 8 5
   ─────────
  1 0 6 5 2
```

Here is a switch—a problem with the digits standing
for letters:

```
      7 6 2
      3 0 0 9
      2 4 8 1
    ─────────
      6 2 5 2
```

The right letters spell out a message. Can you find
the letters?

(*Hint:* Start by using E for 2.)

This is the key:

3 - B
8 - D
2 - E
6 - H
9 - K
4 - N
0 - O
5 - R
1 - S
7 - T

And this is the message: